ON SUBJECTS
OF WHICH
WE KNOW NOTHING

KAREN CARCIA

ON SUBJECTS
OF WHICH
WE KNOW NOTHING

KAREN CARCIA

NEW MICHIGAN PRESS
TUCSON, ARIZONA

NEW MICHIGAN PRESS

DEPT OF ENGLISH, P. O. BOX 210067

UNIVERSITY OF ARIZONA

TUCSON, AZ 85721-0067

<http://newmichiganpress.com/nmp>

Orders and queries to nmp@thediagram.com.

ISBN 978-1-934832-30-1. FIRST PRINTING.

Printed in the United States of America.

Design by Ander Monson.

Cover image by Gaylord Schanilec: birch end-grain
print from *Sylvæ*, Midnight Paper Sales, 2007.

CONTENTS

Poems

Notes

POEMS

ON SUBJECTS OF WHICH WE KNOW NOTHING[1]

Children of the Survivors of Lightning Strikes[2]

Everything illuminated. Oranges and orange rinds,
lemons and lemon rinds, the bright white bitter pith.

The Blind as Drawn by Children

They are lit from within—halos surround their entire
bodies—they become stars and moons in outer space,
drawn, as they are, always on black paper[3].

Sung[4] Pottery

We think of flutes, of drums—wind through small
instruments[5], carried at night under the split moon. We
think of blue and green glazes[6], fish and flags[7], strung
from cart to cart[8] [9].

What Expecting Dying at the Movies Adds to Any
Film[10]

Every word is for you[11]. Embrace the heroine. Hear out
your brother as he confesses by the edge of the lake.
Look long into the lake. Contemplate the moonlight as
it arrives on shore[12], wave upon wave. Ask your heart to
break and it will.

The Rest in Music[13]

How can there be, amongst all that darkness, any moon in the *Moonlight Sonata*[14]? Notes erode those flat, dark trees, no branches interlocking, no swamp to rise from, no dark hillside, no hillside[15].

BY RAINCLOUD OR ANVIL

the night got dark / millimeter by millimeter // it could
not be measured by anything[1] / except absence / like all
matter[2]/ that matters // made more so by the neighbor's
broken door and someone / hammering on it all day to
try / and make the lock catch / I turn up the music //
I'm listening to that song[3]/ again / which is even sadder
once / I realize it's not a duet / but one voice / raised a
few octaves / to sing the lover's part / and that's where
the song becomes / abstract[4] like the layering of shadow
on shadow // lamp black over jet / strike plate over
latch // won't quite catch

STUDY: 930 MINOR[1] AVENUE, NORTH-FACING WINDOW

Gravity[2] makes its slow work known here: the glass
in waves down the window[3]. The grass outside,

the lone rose climbing the weathered wooden fence,
the dried sweet pea[4] vines: all amplified. All real[5] and

not real as seen through this frame[6], as seen
through this memory. The sweet peas exist: now[7]:

as green and pink against the fence. Now[8]: dry.
They exist[9] now for someone else to look out upon.

NOTES ON CHAPTER 4

Visible…desirable. This particular inflorescence[1] says
what about the woodland flowers[2]—says what about
the word for the block of wood from which a bell is
hung[3]—says *some things need more*: white winter wheat
berries. There is no better way. What ways views from
car windows differ from views from house windows—
that instant keening[4]—has not been documented.
Neither has the idea of applepicking: we did that when[5],
we did that why—[6]. If we feel a day so heavenly it could
not end, so we feel we will not[7].

SELECTION[1]

When I begin to map it out, I already see

      how I've left your house out—as if you have no

place to go back to[2]—no place to start from—you're just there

      on the street—in the middle of traffic (going both ways)

so be careful. This map is driven by potential theory[3]—my house,

      myself[4], careening you closer in all the typical

reckless ways of gravity.

                         I may have missed a light on

Jackson, but I drew in the railroad, though you'll see the broken

      down traincar[5] before you cross the tracks. The map

is not to scale, it leaves out the leaving[6], the stove, and the

      current that pushes you along--disturbing

the air, creating a harmonic movement[7] against the tone of my day—.

      By the time you get here, the light will have faded, the clouds

lined up in neat stacks[8], you won't notice the slight awkward arc

      of my roofline, you won't see the dog on the porch,

won't notice the light unhooking itself from the eaves, roofs, trees,

      the very earth itself—.

EPHEMERA

These days apart[1]   a part of me fallen away
　　　like that wind-blown

over

　　　the old motel

and you   broken violin string[2]

　　　you named hours[3]

alone.

　　Don't you remember[4] the way the clouds
　　　set and set over the peaked roof—

each division
　　　　　　　　offers distinction

　　　　　　　　　　　　　　　—

don't you go

　　　　and remember[5]

EDGE

The most silent[1] [2] thing in this suburban night
    where the sky opens in angles[3] above us:

the rabbit I scare from the stairs. It believes
    in a stillness that is practically invisible[4]

under the lullaby[5] of the leaves rubbing together,
    distant windchimes and the dog tag

jangle at the end of this leash. It is not tricked
    by the lit doorways and quietness

of shadows shook[6] across the lawns. Its fear
    so complete in this moment,

not unlike my own, not knowing which
    way to turn in these realms

of silence and uncreated things[7]—so it just[8]
    holds on. Holds still.

DEAR REMEMBERED¹—

What can I tell you of this moment?² As I write, my
lamp erases part of the night. Well, erases my vision of
it. As I write the sky³ remains the same x⁴ blue of ten
o'clock—difference palpable only in the placement of
the moon—a little to the left of where I left it. Waning.
Soon the sky will be emptied of it. Of course, we think
of emptiness more as presence, don't we? An absence
so large it fills things up⁵ ⁶ . Do you have nights like
this there⁷? Nights you're awake, no one else in sight,
and you feel that fullness. Of what?—the vast earth⁸,
I guess. And then the first calls of morning birds⁹, the
car driving by that does not stop, is not filled with your
beloved, so fills the earth with the sound it leaves: gravel
under tire scratching out the way¹⁰.

WHAT I'VE FORGOTTEN

I

Not the ocean and its endless wresting. Not the streets of Gloucester[1]. Not the idea of rain before rain is even forecast. Not the flower named after my friend[2], and not the flower named after no one I know[3]. Not the song[4] covered by the inferior group. Not the man trapped up the telephone pole or the dog who trapped him. Not the Third Street apartment door (which was always unlocked). Not the windswept scape and what I left there[5]. Not the mud on the shore of the curved bank before we dove in.

II

Not the view from our old kitchen window[6]: snow, tangled sweet peas, faded flags—the flat-tack sense of time suspended—black cat on the sky blue car. Not the shape of your knuckles on the stick shift. Not the neon pink of the Capri-Drive-in. Not the windy roads we just took back then[7].

III

Not when I realized I'd never really heard anyone yell until I heard a neighbor yell: "Get out! Get the fuck

out!" to some former former. And not the silence in the
neighborhood after[8]—how it lasted for hours.

IV

Not the wrought iron sign of Rose Cemetery or the
walk through the graveyard to the Crescent Donut shop
because, for once, and for one short moment, we're the
living.

NOTES

NOTES ON "ON SUBJECTS OF WHICH
WE KNOW NOTHING"

1 From a letter Emily Dickinson wrote to Otis P. Lord:
"On subjects of which we know nothing…we both
believe and disbelieve a hundred times an Hour, which
keeps believing nimble." Letter writing, of course, is
an activity that requires absence, however temporary.
How we all should long to be absent, to have one fear
for our "sweet Lungs in the crowded Air."

2 The *survivors* of lightning strikes may have lasting
physical, mental and emotional effects—from fernlike
burnmarks to memory loss or shattered teeth. And,
each year, many who are struck by lightning do not
survive. Take, for instance, this news report from
November 10th: "Three people were killed by lightning
at a graveyard on the outskirts of Mexico City while
attending the funeral of a 62 year old man. Rain forced
the participants under a tree. When lightning hit
the tree, all collapsed. One man, a gravedigger, died
instantly."

3 [They look like you and I, drawn by children: lit from
within. halos. entire bodies. stars and moons. drawn as
we are, or want to be].

4 960-1279, alternately, The Song

5 from, for example, the *guanzi*. The oldest bamboo
instrument of China. How can any *wind* instrument
not inspire or sadden? But you, sad oboe, the
landscape disappears when you rest.

6 to make blue glazes: feldspar, flint, whiting; green
glazes: black copper oxide

7 Imagine something like *papel picado*—Mexican cut
paper banners—not so fragile, but that festive.

8 Or imagine something like the sound of bells in wind:
that hollow below. You may imagine Tibetan prayer
flags, their sad history: designs lost to China's cultural
revolution, woodblocks too heavy to carry over the
Himalayas, used as a source of firewood for Chinese
soldiers. Lone *wind horse* glowing red, turning to
ember, floating up over the

9 soloist "Herding Donkeys" as we make our slow way
along, each long note a step.

10 We may assume that being a gravedigger, one is
more prepared to accept the inevitability of death,
though, one may say that of many: poets, doctors,
nurses, insurance salesmen, paper salesmen, gondola
operators, etc., and one would be just as wrong.

11 Every. One.

12 the mechanics of moonlight

13

14 Even the moonlight seen reflected off Lake Lucerne by Ludwig Rellstab, circa 1836.

15 *See* note 13, or alternately, "quasi una Fantasia," *see* note 16

16 "When…going from nothing…towards something…" (John Cage)

NOTES ON "BY RAINCLOUD OR ANVIL"

1 It starts as a few notes on an upright piano, each one held, the tiny vibration echoing out.

2 as with the Universe, more is unknown than known

3 "Undeclared"

4 when the wish itself is so essential: "O Western wind, when wilt thou blow..."

NOTES ON "STUDY: 930 MINOR AVENUE, NORTH-FACING WINDOW"

1 But what is minor about you, street? Look up and see Ursa Minor shining down on you. Oh that Little Bear, despite his diminutive name, is, depending on where you stand on this planet, more visible. And don't forget Polaris shines in you.

2 If the standard equation for gravity is $(G*m_1*m_2) / d^2$, where G = the gravitational constant, m_1 = the mass of my longing, m_2 = the longing of the sweet peas toward me, and d, the distance between us, = 496.97 miles, what is keeping us apart?

3 The thermodynamics of glass disprove this theory; although, it is yet unsettled whether glass is a liquid or solid.

4 Oh, the poisonous beauties: Annie Gilroy, Mollie Rilestone, Flora Norton, Father Cupani.

5 Like real numbers: the rational and irrational, the negative and positive, the cipher.

6 And the "catch" locks into place this: the broken-down blue-bird-colored car parked in the drive, the black cat, the overgrown edges of the lawn. The catch clicks shut the window.

7 And just what is the difference between the present
and the past? If, as Eric Méchoulan states, "...there
is no difference between the nature of memory and
of forgetting...any more than there is a difference
between immediacy and mediation, to the extent
that they repeat each other, but according to different
speeds and rhythms," then every moment is a process
of immediate loss.

8 Perhaps I should just turn to Faulkner: "The past isn't
dead. It isn't even past." So clear in the way I can't let
go even the way the light wraps the tree trunk, the
car wheel (slightly flattened), and the air around the
squirrel's tail.

9 What's there and not there: the evolutionary endpoint
of stars, any invisible light, really, which shines and
pulls us on.

NOTES ON "NOTES ON CHAPTER 4"

1 panicle

2 spring beauty, bee balm, trillium, red chokeberry

3 stock / stok / stoke

4 the geochemistry of joy and longing

5 1990 in upstate New York, Oswego or Owego

6 like 1:39-1:45 of Erin McKeown's "Daisy and
   Prudence"

7 "The heart luxuriates with indifferent things, /
   Wasting its kindliness on stocks and stones, /
   And on the vacant air." (William Wordsworth)

NOTES ON "SELECTION"

1 There is nothing simple about the mapmaker's deft selection. Historical geographer J.B. Harley conceived of maps as having "silences," places and things left out, and revealed how those silences help to divulge authorial perspectives or biases of a particular map.

2 When you close the door behind you—hear that click, walk away—it all disappears, erases itself: the falling-over wire fence, the back porch with its blue glass globe light, the linoleum floor of the slightly offset kitchen, the transom windows, the front room with its glossed hardwoods, the front porch swing, the geraniums, the cement pathway and steps from the sidewalk—all effaced.

3 the contractible curve vanishes

4 "I feel myself in need….and dart from world to world." (George Moses Horton)

5 The train doesn't run now—so the F# A C# of the Leslie S-3BJ air horn warps out only in memory.

6 —like the hurry of bird wings—

7 Like that first moment of rest before the needle
scratches out the first note of Lenny Breau's "But
Beautiful"

8 altocumulus stratiformis undulatus

NOTES ON "EPHEMERA"

1 "...I remembered / the wrecked season...plans of salvage, / snow, the closed door...machinery of sorrow." (Muriel Rukeyser)

2 threads of wire, an errant e string

3 Yellow Yawn, All Summer, Summerour, Bell's Favorite, Neverfail

4 plan of / for—what one is intending to do; blueprint according to which something is to be done

5 "...and so and also. And also and so and so and also." (Gertrude Stein)

NOTES ON "EDGE"

1 not *marked by absence*, but more silent still from its very presence

2 *see* note 13 from "Notes on "On Subjects Of Which We Know Nothing""

3 the roofline with its shingled gables, the cracking branches of the stick oak tree

4 "What if darkness became unhinged right now?" (John Ashbery)

5 L'était une poule brune / Qu'allait ponder sur la lune / Pondait un p'tit' coco / Que l'enfant mangeait tout chaud.

6 like rugs batted out with elegant Amish hoops, all that heavenly dust of ourselves already passing out of this world

7 Orpheus: "I implore you by these abodes full of terror, these realms of silence and uncreated things, unite again the thread of Eurydice's life."

8 that is, barely

NOTES ON "DEAR REMEMBERED—"

1 This address: so intimate, yet so anonymous. Often
   used by Dickinson who also included admonishments
   to her "remembered": "Do write me soon…and let it
   be a long—long letter…," and perhaps the most arrant,
   "mind me."

2 As Werner Heisenberg says, "In principle, we
   can not know the present in full. Therefore, all
   observation is a selection from a complete domain of
   possibilities…" And as we know from his Uncertainty
   Principle, we cannot know how any letter will be
   received; all we know is that, if received, it will create
   some disturbance, and that disturbance will be
   unpredictable.

3 As I write *the sky* half of the crickets are rubbing out
   their calling songs. Using Dolbear's law, $T = 50 \frac{N-40}{4}$,
   where N equals the number of cricket chirps per
   minute, it must be $77°$.

4 Imagine cerulean blue, so useful for atmospheric
   shading; or, the blue of Rothko's "Greens and Blue on
   Blue," 1956; the blue of the first ocean you ever swam
   in—not quite as blue as you'd imagined, but there,
   glinting up through the waves.

5 Stanley Plumly writes of "To Autumn": "…that ever so
much, ever so little, loss adds up to more, fills more,
empties more, than the heart of the harvest."

6 empty glasses left on nightstands, the air in seaside
towns

7 Most letters have one intended, one, perhaps, who
lives in Denver, Colorado.

8 Ulan-Ude, Katete, Eights Station, Songsong, wood
ear mushroom, peach rust, tath, bonobo, giraffe,
cinnamon, sorrel, nevermind the mitral valve that
lies between the left atrium and left ventricle of the
human heart.

9 The tufted titmouse, for instance, calling for my father
to get up out of the dream of my father's name: *peter
peter peter*; or the black-throated green warbler
arching out its landscape: *trees-trees-murmuring-trees.*

10 Wait, one cricket has found its mate—yes, listen, he's
singing his quiet courting song now.

NOTES ON "WHAT I'VE FORGOTTEN"

1 and that day—the streets and sky the same slate
  gray—I wasn't supposed to be there with you

2 Sweet William

3 Zinnia—named after Johann Gottfried Zinn, who
  also has a part of the eye named after him

4 "Strangers"

5 the unnameable

6 For more on this window-view *see* "Study: 930 Minor
  Avenue, North-facing Window."

7 beauty expressed in a sigh

8 under the stung air—all of us—stunned—every bird
  and blade of grass, every word

ACKNOWLEDGMENTS

A version of "Notes on Chapter 4" first appeared in
Born Magazine.

"By Raincloud or Anvil," "Dear Remembered—,"
"Notes on 'By Raincloud or Anvil,'" and "Notes on 'Dear
Remembered—'" first appeared in *DIAGRAM.*

THANKS

Many thanks to Joan & Peter Carcia and Vivian & John D'Agostino. And thanks to Kathy Carcia Gibson, Anthony Carcia, Shannon Brazil, Carrie Rohman, Renee Takara, and Mary Louise Poe Smith.

Special thanks to Ander Monson, Nancy Eimers, Bill Olsen, Dobby Gibson, Allegra Blake, Marcel Brouwers, and Matt Hart. Thanks also to Mary Ruefle, Dean Young, David Wojahn, Roger Mitchell, Cornelia Nixon, Maura Stanton, Daneen Wardrop, Herb Scott, Stu Dybek, Gwen Raaberg, Peter Blickle, Jaimy Gordon, Cynthia Running-Johnson, Susan Swartwout, Barb Jenkins, Kirsten Hemmy, Alex Long, Billy Reynolds, David Daniels, Scott Stubbs, Cole Windler, Perrey Lee, Sara Langworthy, Sara Sauers, Julie Leonard, Matt Brown, Gaylord Schanilec, Bob Gates, and Ann Mottl.

David Daniels is my "Dear Remembered." "Edge" is for Amelia Bird.

This book is for Jamie.

COLOPHON

Text is set in a digital version of Jenson, designed by Robert Slimbach in 1996, and based on the work of punchcutter, printer, and publisher Nicolas Jenson.

KAREN CARCIA grew up in Reading, Massachusetts. She took an M.F.A. in creative writing from Indiana University and a Ph.D. in English from Western Michigan University. Her poems have appeared in *Absent; Born Magazine; Conduit; DIAGRAM; Forklift, Ohio; FIELD; Fine Madness; Hunger Mountain;* and *Salt Hill Journal.* Currently she is a Research Assistant at the University of Iowa Center for the Book.

⌐⌐

NEW MICHIGAN PRESS, based in Tucson, Arizona, prints poetry and prose chapbooks, especially work that transcends traditional genre. Together with DIAGRAM, NMP sponsors a yearly chapbook competition.

DIAGRAM, a journal of text, art, and schematic, is published bimonthly at THEDIAGRAM.COM. Periodic print anthologies are available from the New Michigan Press at NEWMICHIGANPRESS.COM/NMP.

CPSIA information can be obtained at www.ICGtesting.com
Printed in the USA
BVOW070635060112

279928BV00001B/3/P

9 781934 832301